C000282731

■ Flute

THE ELENA DURAN COLLECTION 2 for flute & piano VOLUME 1 Grades 1–2

Little Gems

Original pieces by John Lenehan
Edited and presented by Elena Durán

ED 12768
ISMN M-2201-2459-4

www.schott-music.com

Mainz ● London ● Madrid ● New York ● Paris ● Prague ● Tokyo ● Toronto

ED 12768
British Library Cataloguing-in-Publication Data.
A catalogue record for this book is available from the British Library
ISMN M-2201-2459-4

French translation: Agnès Ausseur
German translation: Ute Corleis
Spanish translation: José Luis Chávez
Cover design and page layout by Russell Stretten Consultancy
Music setting and page layout by Jackie Leigh
Printed in Germany S&Co.8106

Contents / Sommaire / Inhalt / Contenido

Foreword

I have always loved gemstones and wherever I go in the world on tour I go looking for them. When I was last in Australia a friend took me to a mine to see the most amazing stones being opened from their natural rock – what a wonderful experience! It was at that moment that I decided to make a collection of Little Gems in a book for flute players who want something a bit different. I have specifically focused on birthstones because they are universal: we all have birthdays and love to acknowledge them in different ways.

Gemstones have a remarkable history that goes back as far as the first century AD, and the Roman, Jewish and Russian cultures have all favoured different combinations. The custom as we know it today, however, only became popular during the eighteenth century, starting first in Poland and afterwards spreading throughout Europe and the rest of the world.

For *Little Gems* I have chosen the most popular stones and listed some historical and mythological insights alongside their more well-known attributes. You might enjoy researching other traits, such as the psychological, mental, emotional and healing aspects of these wonderful gemstones!

I hope you enjoy the variety, colour and meaning of these beautiful little flute pieces, which truly are little gems in themselves and were composed especially for you by John Lenehan.

Elena

Préface

J'ai toujours aimé les pierres précieuses et j'en rapporte de toutes les régions du monde dans lesquelles je voyage. Lors de mon dernier séjour en Australie, un ami m'a emmenée visiter une mine et assister à l'extraction des pierres les plus extraordinaires de leur gangue naturelle. Quel moment inoubliable ! C'est à ce moment que je décidai de rassembler un recueil de *Petites gemmes* pour les flûtistes avides d'expériences un peu différentes. Je me suis limitée aux pierres bénéfiques associées à chaque mois de naissance car elles sont universelles : chacun aime fêter son anniversaire à sa façon.

L'usage des pierres précieuses remonte au premier siècle de notre ère et au cours de l'histoire, les cultures romaine, juive et russe ont toutes eu recours à différentes combinaisons de gemmes. Toutefois, la coutume telle que nous la connaissons aujourd'hui se propagea pendant le XVIIIe siècle depuis la Pologne à travers l'Europe et le reste du monde.

Pour ce recueil de *Petites gemmes*, j'ai choisi les pierres les plus connues et donné quelques détails sur leur histoire et leur passé mythologique, ainsi que sur leurs attributs les plus célèbres. A vous de rechercher d'autres aspects psychologiques, psychiques, émotionnels et curatifs associés à ces merveilleuses pierres !

J'espère que vous apprécierez la diversité, la couleur et le sens de chacune de ces pièces brèves pour la flûte, véritable joyaux composés pour vous par John Lenehan.

Elena

Vorwort

Solange ich denken kann, liebe ich Edelsteine und wo auch immer in der Welt ich auf Konzertreise gehe, suche ich nach ihnen. Als ich kürzlich in Australien war, nahm mich ein Freund in eine Mine mit, um mir die erstaunlichsten Steine zu zeigen, nachdem sie aus dem Naturstein herausgelöst worden waren – was für eine wunderbare Erfahrung! In diesem Moment beschloss ich, ein Sammlung von Little Gems (= Kleine Edelsteine) in einem Buch zusammenzutragen, und zwar für Flötisten, die ein bisschen das Besondere wollen. Den Schwerpunkt habe ich auf Geburtssteine gelegt, weil sie universal sind: wir haben alle Geburtstag und feiern ihn gerne auf unterschiedliche Art und Weise.

Die Edelsteine haben eine bemerkenswerte Geschichte, die bis ins erste Jahrhundert n. Chr. zurückgeht, und die römischen, jüdischen und russischen Kulturen bevorzugten alle unterschiedliche Kombinationen. Der Brauch, wie wir ihn kennen, wurde allerdings erst im 18. Jahrhundert beliebt. Er begann in Polen und breitete sich danach in ganz Europa und dem Rest der Welt aus.

Für Little Gems habe ich die beliebtesten Steine ausgewählt und zusätzlich zu ihren bekannteren Eigenschaften habe ich einige geschichtliche und mythologische Einblicke aufgelistet. Vielleicht macht es dir ja Spaß, noch andere Aspekte herauszufinden, wie z.B. den psychologischen, geistigen, emotionalen oder heilenden Aspekt.

Ich hoffe, du wirst die Vielfältigkeit, Farbe und Bedeutung dieser schönen kleinen Flötenstücke genießen. Sie sind wirklich kleine Edelsteine in sich und wurden von John Lenehan speziell für dich komponiert.

Elena

Prólogo

Siempre he amado las piedras preciosas y dondequiera que voy de gira en el mundo las busco. La última vez que estuve en Australia un amigo me llevó a una mina para ver las piedras más asombrosas al ser extraidas de la roca natural – ¡qué experiencia tan maravillosa! Fue en ese momento que decidí hacer una colección de Pequeñas Gemas en un libro para los flautistas que quieren algo un poco diferente. Me he concentrado específicamente en gemas asociadas a la fecha de nuestro nacimiento porque son universales: todos tenemos cumpleaños y amamos reconocerlos de diversas maneras.

Las piedras preciosas tienen una notable historia que se remonta tan lejos como el siglo primero D.C., y las culturas romanas, judias y rusas favorecieron diferentes combinaciones. Sin embargo, la costumbre, como la conocemos ahora, se popularizó en el siglo dieciocho, comenzando primero en Polonia y pasando luego a través de Europa y el resto del mundo.

Para Pequeñas Gemas he elegido las piedras más populares y he enumerado algunas interpretaciones históricas y mitológicas, así como algunas de las cualidades más conocidas de cada una. ¡Usted puede disfrutar investigando otros aspectos tales como los aspectos psicologicos, mentales, emocionales y curativos de estas maravillosas piedras preciosas!

Deseo que usted goce de la variedad, el color y el significado de estas pequeñas y bellas piezas para flauta, que son en verdad pequeñas gemas en sí mismas y fueron compuestas especialmente para usted por John Lenehan.

Elena

Gemstone

Warm-ups are very important. Many flautists have routines that they follow every time they begin their work and **Gemstone** is one such example that you can play each day at the beginning of your practice. Keep your air-stream relaxed yet focused. During the rests make sure you loosen your whole body and re-balance the instrument in your hands. Long notes are especially important in developing your overall control, so enjoy them!

L'échauffement est essentiel. De nombreux flûtistes reprennent certains exercices chaque fois qu'ils se mettent au travail et **Gemstone** *est un exercice que vous pouvez intégrer chaque jour au début de votre pratique. Gardez un souffle très détendu mais concentré. Pensez à relâcher les mains, la tête et le corps pendant les silences et à rééquilibrer l'instrument entre vos mains. Soignez les notes longues, très importantes pour le développement général et la maîtrise.*

Das Aufwärmen ist sehr wichtig. Viele Flötisten haben Routineübungen, mit denen sie jedes Mal ihre Arbeit beginnen, und **Gemstone** *ist solch ein Beispiel, mit dem du jeden Tag dein Üben beginnen kannst. Bemühe dich um einen entspannten aber fokussierten Luftstrom. Achte darauf, dass du in den Pausen deinen ganzen Körper entspannst und das Instrument in deinen Händen neu ausbalancierst. Lange Noten sind besonders wichtig dafür, eine Gesamtkontrolle zu entwickeln - genieße sie also!*

Los calentamientos son muy importantes. Muchos flautistas tienen rutinas que hacen cuando empiezan su trabajo cada vez y la **Piedra Preciosa** es una rutina que usted puede hacer cada día al principio de su práctica. Mantenga su corriente de aire muy relajada pero enfocada. Durante el resto afloje completamente su cuerpo y reequilibre el instrumento en sus manos. Las notas largas son muy importantes al desarrollar su control de manera total ¡así que disfrútelas!

Light the Spirit

Garnet – January

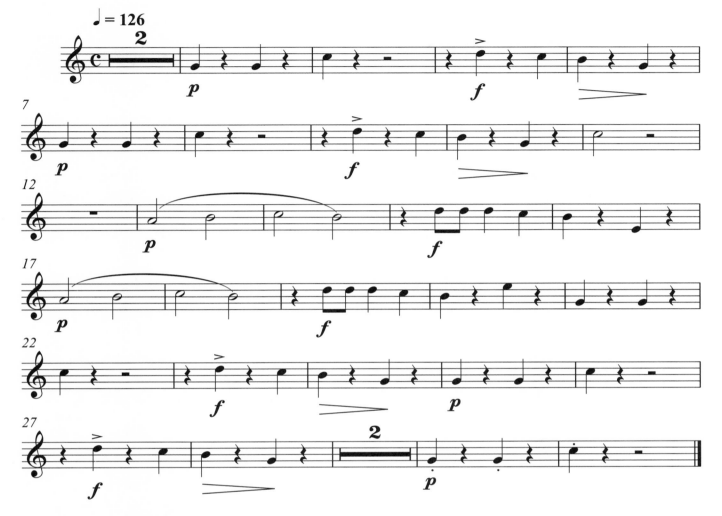

The name '**garnet**' is believed to come from the Latin *punica granatum*, meaning 'pomegranate stone', because of its resemblance to the seed of that fruit. Garnet is an energiser and motivator. It sharpens your perceptions, opens your heart and bestows self-confidence. Its sources are Slovakia, South Africa, the USA, Australia, Brazil and Sri Lanka – a truly international stone!

A more uplifting style of tone is required here so play each note with a positive resonance.

*Man glaubt, dass sich der Name **Granat** von dem lateinischen Begriff punica granatum, was Granatapfelstein bedeutet, herleitet, wegen seiner Ähnlichkeit mit dem Samen dieser Frucht. Der Granat ist ein Energiespender und wirkt belebend. Er schärft deine Wahrnehmung, öffnet dein Herz und verleiht Selbstvertrauen. Fundstellen sind die Slowakei, Südafrika, die USA, Australien, Brasilien und Sri Lanka – ein wahrlich internationaler Stein!*

Hier wird eine eher erhebende Tonfärbung verlangt. Spiele daher jede Note mit einem vollen, positiven Klang.

*Le nom du **grenat** viendrait du latin punica granatum, ou pierre de grenade, du fait de sa ressemblance avec les graines de ce fruit. Le grenat est un énergisant et un stimulant qui aiguise les perceptions, ouvre le cœur et augmente la confiance en soi. On le trouve en Slovaquie, en Afrique du Sud, aux Etats-Unis, en Australie, au Brésil et au Sri Lanka – une pierre très internationale !*

Un ton d'un style plus enlevé est de mise ici et suppose de jouer chaque note avec une résonance nette.

El nombre **granate** se cree que proviene del latín *punica granatum*, que significa piedra de la Granada, debido a su semejanza a la semilla de esa fruta. El granate es un activador y un motivador. Agudiza sus percepciones, abre su corazón y concede confianza en sí mismo. Sus fuentes son Eslovaquia, Sudáfrica, los Estados Unidos, Australia, Brasil y Sri Lanka – ¡una piedra verdaderamente internacional!

Un estilo de tono más inspirado se requiere aquí para tocar cada nota con una resonancia positiva.

Go Forth!

Amethyst – February

The **amethyst** is a popular semiprecious stone that has adorned jewellery for at least 5,000 years. It was used by the ancient Egyptians and became popular in both classical Greece and Rome. The Romans even included the stone in a myth involving Bacchus (the god of wine and ecstasy) and the young maiden Amethistos. About to be attacked by wild animals, Amethistos prayed to the moon goddess Diana, who turned her into stone. When Bacchus discovered the transformed girl, he poured wine over her stone body and the statue turned to amethyst.

Amethyst is a stone of the mind and evokes calm and clarity. It is one of the most spiritual stones and is said to enhance memory and improve motivation. Perfect for the flute player!

Pay attention to the phrasing and concentrate hard during the quicker passages. Listen carefully to the piano part at bar 22, then 'go forth' to a peaceful and soft ending.

L'améthyste est une pierre semi-précieuse très populaire qui orne les bijoux depuis au moins cinq mille ans. Pendant l'Antiquité, les Egyptiens puis les Grecs et les Romains l'ont beaucoup utilisée. La mythologie romaine la relie à Bacchus, dieu du vin et de l'extase, et à la jeune Amethistos. Alors qu'elle allait être attaquée par des bêtes sauvages, Amethistos implora Diane, déesse de la Lune, qui la transforma en pierre. Bacchus, découvrant la jeune fille pétrifiée, versa du vin sur elle et la métamorphosa en améthyste.

L'améthyste est la pierre de l'esprit, elle représente le calme et la clarté. C'est une des pierres à forte charge spirituelle réputée favoriser la mémoire et améliorer la motivation. Parfaite pour les flûtistes !

Faites attention au phrasé et concentrez-vous tout particulièrement sur les notes rapides. Ecoutez attentivement le piano à la mesure 22 et « en avant ! » vers une conclusion paisible et douce.

*Der **Amethyst** ist ein beliebter Halbedelstein, der seit mindestens 5000 Jahren Schmuck geziert hat. Er wurde von den alten Ägyptern benutzt und war sowohl im antiken Griechenland als auch in Rom beliebt. Die Römer machten den Stein sogar zu einem Teil eines Mythos über Bacchus (den Gott des Weines und der Ekstase) und die Jungfrau Amethistos. Als wilde Tiere diese gerade angreifen wollten, betete Amethistos zu der Mondgöttin, die sie in einen Stein verwandelte. Als Bacchus jedoch das Mädchen entdeckte, schüttete er Wein über den zu Stein gewordenen Körper und die Statue verwandelte sich in einen Amethyst.*

Der Amethyst ist ein Stein des Geistes und bringt Ruhe und Klarheit. Er ist einer der spirituellen Steine, und man sagt ihm eine Verbesserung des Gedächtnisses und der Motivation nach. Perfekt für den Flötisten!

Beachte die Phrasierung und konzentriere dich besonders während der schnelleren Passagen. Höre dir den Klavierpart in Takt 22 besonders sorgfältig an und strebe dann vorwärts (= go forth) zu einem friedlichen und weichen Ende.

La **amatista** es una popular piedra semipreciosa, que ha adornado la joyería por lo menos 5000 años. Fue utilizada por los egipcios antiguos y era popular en la Grecia y Roma clásicas. Los romanos incluyeron esta piedra en un mito que envolvia a Baco (el dios del vino y del éxtasis) y la joven virgen Amethistos. A punto de ser atacada por los animales salvajes, Amethistos rezó a Diana, diosa de la Luna, quien la convirtió en piedra. Sin embargo, cuando Baco descubrió a la joven transformada, derramó vino sobre su cuerpo petrificado y la estatua se convirtió en amatista.

La amatista es una piedra de la mente y trae calma y claridad. Es una de las piedras más espirituales, realza la memoria y mejora la motivación. ¡Perfecta para el flautista!

Ponga atención al fraseo y especial cuidado a las notas más rápidas. Escuche cuidadosamente la parte del piano en la barra 22 y entonces vaya 'adelante' hacia a un tranquilo y suave final.

Sea Breeze

Aquamarine – March

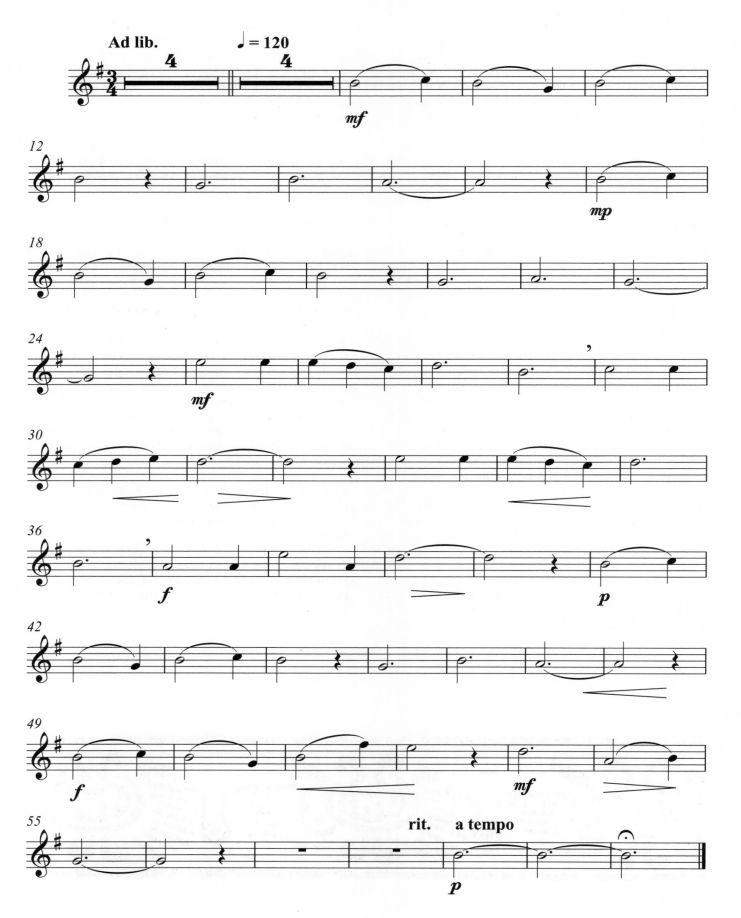

Aquamarine is the precious, clear blue-green variety of the mineral beryl. It is considered to be the stone of courage and also has cleansing properties due to its connection with the purity of water. The stone was enjoyed as long ago as the third century BC and, together with images of Poseidon (the god of the seas) with his trident, the Greeks and Romans used it as a protective charm for overseas journeys. This positive gemstone is a symbol of happiness and hope, and it has also been associated with love and friendship.

Pay particular attention to the special introduction. Strive for a really consistent legato when you have the slurs and an even air-stream on the long notes (especially the last one).

*L'**aigue-marine** est la variété précieuse, de couleur bleu-vert, du béryl. Elle est réputée être la pierre du courage et avoir des propriétés purificatrices grâce à ses liens avec l'eau. On l'utilisait déjà au troisième siècle avant notre ère et les Grecs et les Romains s'en servaient comme amulette protectrice, jointe à des images de Poséidon, le dieu de la mer au trident, lors de leurs voyages au-delà des mers. Cette pierre bienfaisante, symbole de bonheur et d'espoir, est également associée à l'amour et à l'amitié.*

Attention à cette introduction très singulière ! Efforcez-vous de réaliser un legato constant pendant les liaisons de phrasé et maintenez un souffle égal sur les notes tenues, surtout sur la dernière.

*Der **Aquamarin** ist die kostbare, glasklare blaugrüne Ausprägung des Minerals Beryll. Man betrachtet ihn als Stein des Mutes, er hat aber auch reinigende Kräfte auf Grund seiner Verbindung mit der Reinheit des Wassers. Er wird bereits seit dem 3. Jahrhundert v. Chr. eingesetzt. Zusammen mit Bildern von Poseidon (dem Gott der Weltmeere) und seinem Dreizack benutzten ihn sowohl die Griechen als auch die Römer als Schutzzauber bei Überseereisen. Dieser positive Edelstein ist ein Symbol für Glück und Hoffnung und wird auch mit Liebe und Freundschaft in Verbindung gebracht.*

Beachte vor allem die besondere Einleitung. Bemühe dich bei den Bindungen sehr um ein einheitliches, dichtes Legato und einen gleichmäßigen Atemstrom auf den langen Noten – besonders der letzten.

El **aguamarina** es la preciosa variedad azulverde clara del mineral berilio. Se le considera ser la piedra del valor, y también tiene características de limpieza debido a su conexión con la pureza del agua. La piedra fue disfrutada desde tiempos tan remotos como el siglo tercero A.C. y, junto con las imágenes de Poseidón (el dios de los mares) con su tridente, griegos y romanos utilizaron la piedra como encanto protector para los viajes de ultramar. Esta positiva piedra preciosa es un símbolo de la felicidad y de la esperanza y también se le asocia con el amor y la amistad.

Ponga particular atención a la introducción especial. Esfuércese para lograr un legato realmente constante cuando ejecute los ligados y una corriente de aire uniforme en las notas largas (especialmente la última).

Sparkle

Diamond – April

April's birthstone is known for its incredible hardness, and the name '**diamond**' is derived from the Greek word *adamas*, meaning 'unconquerable'. The diamond was first discovered over 2000 years ago and mainly came from river gravel in India, although today the gem comes from more than twenty countries. Diamonds can be clear white, yellow, blue, brown or even pink! This diverse stone is rare and acts as a symbol of purity. Mentally, diamonds provide a link between the intellect and the higher mind. They bring clarity to the senses and aid enlightenment: the perfect stone for the flute player!

Work towards a really positive sounding staccato. Make the articulation precise and try to be very accurate so that you attain a real sparkle!

*Der Geburtsstein des Monats April ist für seine unglaubliche Härte bekannt. Der Name **Diamant** leitet sich von dem griechischen Wort* adamas *her, das ‚unbesiegbar' bedeutet. Der Diamant wurde vor über 2000 Jahren entdeckt und wurde damals hauptsächlich als Flusskiesel in Indien geschürft, obwohl er heutzutage in mehr als zwanzig Ländern vorkommt. Diamanten können rein weiß, gelb, blau, braun oder sogar rosa sein! Dieser vielfältige Stein ist selten und steht als Symbol für die Reinheit. In geistiger Hinsicht stellen Diamanten eine Verbindung zwischen dem Intellekt und der höheren Geistesebene dar. Sie bringen den Sinnen Klarheit und verhelfen zur Erleuchtung: der perfekte Stein für den Flötisten!*

Arbeite auf einen wirklich positiv klingenden Stakkatoton hin. Spiele die Artikulation präzise und versuche, sehr genau zu sein, um ein echtes Funkeln zu erhalten!

*Le nom du **diamant** est dérivé du mot grec* adamas, *signifiant invincible, du fait de l'incroyable dureté de cette magnifique pierre, découverte il y a plus de deux mille ans. Essentiellement extrait, à l'origine, des graviers du fond des rivières indiennes, le diamant provient de nos jours de plus de vingt pays. D'un blanc transparent, de couleur jaune, bleue, brune ou même rose, cette pierre rare aux aspects divers est le symbole de la pureté. Du côté psychique, le diamant, qui fait le lien entre l'intellectualité et l'esprit, favorise discernement et sagesse et se révèle la pierre parfaite pour les flûtistes !*

Travaillez dans le sens d'un staccato *bien affirmé. Efforcez-vous à la rigueur du phrasé et à la plus grande précision pour ainsi obtenir un véritable scintillement !*

La piedra de cumpleaños de Abril es conocida por su increible dureza, y el nombre "**diamante**" se deriva de la palabra griega *adamas,* que significa "invincible". El diamante fue descubierto hace más de 2000 años y vino principalmente de la grava de los ríos en la India aunque, los diamantes provienen hoy de más de veinte países. ¡Los diamantes pueden ser blancos claros, amarillos, azules, marrones o aún rosados! Esta diversa piedra es rara y es un símbolo de pureza. Mentalmente, los diamantes proporcionan un acoplamiento entre el intelecto y la mente más elevada. Trae la claridad de la mente y ayuda a la iluminación: ¡la piedra perfecta para el flautista!

Trabaje para lograr un staccato que suene realmente positivo. ¡Ejecute la articulación de manera exacta e intente ser muy preciso para obtener una verdadera chispa!

Day Dreamer

Emerald – May

THE ELENA DURAN COLLECTION 2 for flute & piano **VOLUME 1 Grades 1–2**

Little Gems

Original pieces by John Lenehan
Edited and presented by Elena Durán

ED 12768
ISMN M-2201-2459-4

www.schott-music.com

Mainz ● London ● Madrid ● New York ● Paris ● Prague ● Tokyo ● Toronto

Contents / Sommaire / Inhalt / Contenido

ED 12768
British Library Cataloguing-in-Publication Data.
A catalogue record for this book is available from the British Library
ISMN M-2201-2459-4

French translation: Agnès Ausseur
German translation: Ute Corleis
Spanish translation: José Luis Chávez
Cover design and page layout by Russell Stretten Consultancy
Music setting and page layout by Jackie Leigh
Printed in Germany S&Co.8106

Gemstone

Light the Spirit

Garnet – January

Go Forth!

Amethyst – February

Sea Breeze

Aquamarine – March

Sparkle

Diamond – April

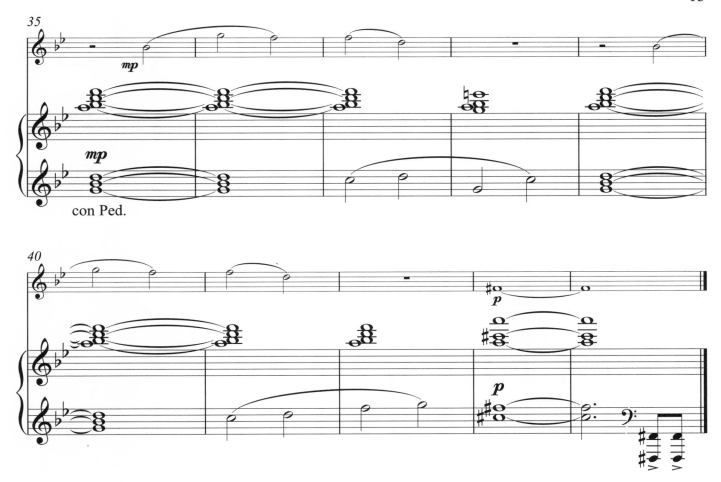

Day Dreamer

Emerald – May

Purity

Pearl – June

The Serpent

Ruby – July

The Stone

Moonstone – August

Cool Blues

Sapphire – September

Illusion

Opal – October

Golden Rays

Topaz – November

Sacred Song

Turquoise – December

The Ancient Egyptians mined **emeralds** in Koseir, and the stone's association with the life-giving properties of the River Nile was said to be related to its green colour. Many fine emeralds were also brought to Europe by the Spanish after the conquest of the Aztecs.

Honesty, truth and holiness have been said to be connected with the Emerald, and it has also been associated with true love. The rich green colour brings forth the energy of growth, peace, and abundance, and imparts mental clarity, inspiring a deeper inner knowledge – perfect for your practice!

The dual character of this 'air and jig' allows you to play the main melody in two ways. In the first section a beautiful smooth legato is required, but during the quicker section play with a bouncy feel in the air-stream. Don't be afraid to repeat the two sections so that you can compare them.

*Les anciens Egyptiens extrayaient l'**émeraude** à Koseir et son association avec les propriétés génératrices de vie du Nil était, semble-t-il, due à sa couleur verte. De nombreuses émeraudes superbes furent également rapportées en Europe par les Espagnols après leur conquête sur les Aztèques.*

L'honnêteté, la vérité et la sainteté sont les qualités liées à l'émeraude qui est aussi la pierre de l'amour sincère. Sa riche couleur verte fait ressortir l'énergie de la croissance, la paix et l'abondance. Elle procure également la perspicacité mentale et inspire la connaissance en profondeur. Parfaite pour votre travail !

Les deux parties de cet « air et gigue » permettent d'interpréter son thème principal selon deux caractères différents. La première section réclame un beau legato lisse tandis que la deuxième section, plus rapide, exige un effet de rebondissement dans le souffle. N'hésitez pas à reprendre les deux parties pour bien les opposer.

*Die alten Ägypter bauten **Smaragde** in Koseir ab. Die Verbindung mit den Leben spendenden Kräften des Nils sagt man ihm wegen seiner grünen Farbe nach. Von den Spaniern wurden auch viele schöne Smaragde nach dem Sieg über die Azteken nach Europa gebracht.*

Man sagt, dass Ehrlichkeit, Treue und Heiligkeit mit dem Smaragd verbunden sind, aber auch wahre Liebe. Die reiche grüne Farbe unterstützt besonders die Energie des Wachstums, des Friedens und der Fülle. Darüber hinaus vermittelt er geistige Klarheit und weckt ein tiefes inneres Wissen – perfekt für dein Training!

Der duale Charakter dieser ,Air und Jig' ermöglicht es dir, die Hauptmelodie auf zwei Arten zu spielen. Im ersten Abschnitt benötigt man ein sehr schönes weiches Legato, aber im schnelleren Abschnitt solltest du mit einem federnden Gefühl im Luftstrom spielen. Wiederhole die beiden Abschnitte ruhig, so dass du sie miteinander vergleichen kannst.

Los antiguos egipcios extrajeron **esmeraldas** en Koseir y su asociación con las propiedades benefactoras de vida del río Nilo se decía eran debida a su color verde. Muchas Esmeraldas finas fueron traídas también a Europa por los españoles después de la conquista de los Aztecas.

La honradez, la verdad y santidad han sido virtudes ligadas con la esmeralda, de quien también se menciona ser una piedra que representa el amor verdadero. El rico color verde refleja la energía del crecimiento, de la paz y de la abundancia. ¡También imparte claridad mental, e inspira un conocimiento interno profundo – ¡perfecto para su práctica!

El carácter de éste "air" y "jig" le permite tocar esta encantadora pieza de dos maneras. La primera sección requiere un hermoso legato, pero durante la sección rápida toque con una sensación de rebote en la corriente de aire. No tema repetir las dos secciones para que las pueda comparar.

Purity

Pearl – June

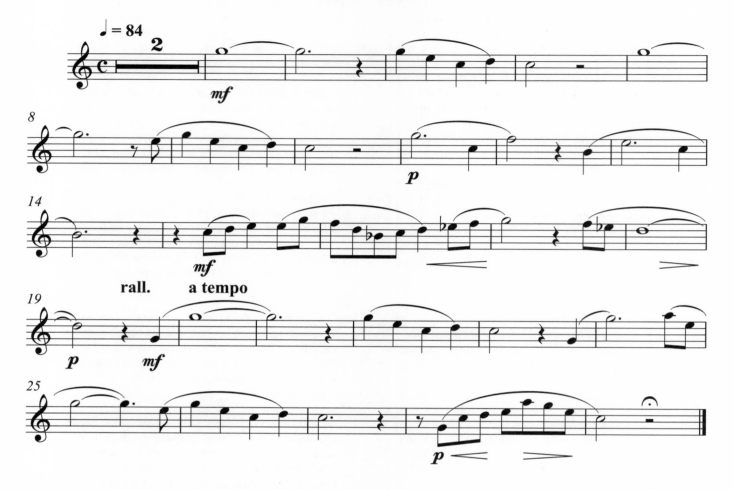

The **pearl** is an organic gemstone derived from shellfish, and its name is thought to have developed from the Latin word *pernula*. This soft gem has little resistance but is nonetheless regarded as a precious stone because of its beauty and rarity. In both China and India the pearl is a symbol of purity, excellence, longevity, immortality, enlightenment and wisdom: no flautist could ask for more!

This gently flowing piece will help you develop the ability to hold very long notes. Be sure to breathe deeply before you play these sections. Keep your sound delicate and tone pure – and don't blow too hard!

Die **Perle** *ist ein organischer Edelstein, der aus Schalentieren stammt. Dieser weiche Stein hat wenig Widerstandsfähigkeit, wird wegen seiner Schönheit und Reinheit aber dennoch als sehr kostbar angesehen. Sowohl in China als auch in Indien ist die Perle ein Symbol von Reinheit, des Besonderen, Langlebigkeit, Unsterblichkeit, Erleuchtung und Weisheit: kein Flötist kann mehr verlangen!*

Das sanft dahinfließende Musikstück wird dir helfen, die Fähigkeit zum Aushalten langer Noten weiterzuentwickeln. Stelle sicher, dass du tief einatmest, bevor du die einzelnen Teile spielst. Der Klang sollte fein und der Ton rein sein – und blase nicht zu kräftig.

La **perle** *est une pierre fine organique provenant des coquillages. Cette pierre offre peu de résistance mais est néanmoins considérée comme précieuse du fait de sa rareté et de sa limpidité. En Chine et en Inde, la perle symbolise la pureté, l'excellence, la longévité, l'immortalité, le discernement et la sagesse. Un flûtiste ne peut demander mieux !*

Cette pièce au flux délicat aidera à développer votre capacité de tenue des notes longues. Prenez une bonne respiration avant de les jouer. Maintenez une sonorité douce et intacte sans souffler trop fort !

La **perla** es una piedra preciosa orgánica que proviene de los crustáceos. Esta suave gema tiene poca resistencia pero no obstante se le tiene como preciosa debido a su rara belleza. En China y la India, la perla es un símbolo de la pureza, de la excelencia, de la longevidad, de la inmortalidad, de la iluminación y de la sabiduría: ¡ningún flautista podía pedir más!

Esta pieza, que fluye amablemente, le ayudará a desarrollar la capacidad de sostener notas muy largas. Esté seguro respirar profundamente antes de tocar estas secciones. Mantenga su sonido delicado y tono puro – ¡y no sople demasiado fuerte!

The Serpent

Ruby – July

In India the **ruby** is the most prized gemstone as it is thought to carry the beneficent energy of the sun, and traditionally it symbolises wealth and power. The ruby is thought to be the stone of the heart and is excellent for your energy levels. It brings about a positive and courageous state of mind and encourages concentration – just what you need for your practice!

Pay attention to the style of the first two bars in the piano and then play with a smooth legato with very even fingers, hardly lifting them from the keys. Make sure that you have a good hand position.

*En Inde, le **rubis** est la pierre la plus prisée car elle est censée rayonner de l'énergie bénéfique du soleil et symbolise traditionnellement la fortune et la puissance. Le rubis, pierre du cœur, est excellente pour stimuler l'entrain, elle procure un état d'esprit positif et courageux et favorise la concentration. Exactement ce dont vous avez besoin dans votre travail !*

Attention aux deux premières mesures du piano ! Imprégnez-vous du style et jouez avec un legato lisse et des doigts très égaux, à peine soulevés des clefs. Assurez-vous de maintenir une bonne position de la main.

*In Indien ist der **Rubin** der wertvollste Edelstein, da man von ihm glaubt, dass er die wohltuende Energie der Sonne in sich trägt und traditionell Reichtum und Macht verkörpert. Der Rubin gilt als Herzstein und ist ein ausgezeichneter Stein für deine Energie. Er unterstützt sowohl einen positiven und mutigen Geisteszustand als auch die Konzentration – also genau das Richtige für dein Training!*

Achte auf den Stil der ersten zwei Takte im Klavier und spiele dann ein weiches Legato mit sehr gleichmäßiger Fingerführung, die sich kaum von den Klappen abhebt. Prüfe nach, ob du eine gute Handposition hast.

En la India el **Rubí** es la piedra preciosa más estimada porque se piensa que trae consigo la benefactora energía del sol, y tradicionalmente simboliza la abundancia y el poder. Se piensa que el Rubí es la piedra del corazón y es una piedra excelente para la energía. Crea un estado de la mente positivo y valeroso. Es una piedra excelente para la concentración – ¡justo lo que necesita su práctica!

Ponga atención a las primeras dos barras del piano, escuchando el estilo, y toque con un buen legato con los dedos muy iguales, levantándolos apenas de las llaves. Cerciórese de tener una buena posición de la mano.

The Stone

Moonstone – August

With its soft gentle sheen, reminiscent of the light cast by the moon, the **moonstone** is said to be the gem of new beginnings. In India the moonstone has always been held in high esteem by women, as it is thought to emphasise female virtues. This reflective stone represents the cycle of change and it also has the powerful effect of calming the emotions.

Look for a different sound by using an absolutely straight air-stream with no vibrato, and enjoy playing a piece with such a distinctive style!

Wegen seines weichen, freundlichen Glanzes, der an das Licht des Mondes erinnert, sagt man vom Mondstein, dass er der Edelstein des Neubeginns ist. In Indien wurde der Mondstein vor allem von den Frauen schon immer sehr geschätzt, da man glaubt, dass er die weiblichen Tugenden fördert. Dieser reflektierende Stein symbolisiert den Kreislauf der Veränderung und hat auch einen sehr stark beruhigenden Effekt auf die Emotionen.

Suche nach einem anderen Klang, indem du einen völlig geraden Luftstrom ohne Vibrato benutzt und genieße es, einmal ein Musikstück mit solch einem unverwechselbaren Stil zu spielen.

*Avec son éclat délicat, rappelant la douce lumière diffusée par la Lune, la **pierre de Lune** évoque les nouveaux départs. En Inde, la pierre de Lune a toujours été très estimée par les femmes car elle est réputée souligner les vertus féminines. Cette pierre méditative, symbolisant le cycle de l'évolution, est très efficace pour calmer les émotions.*

Recherchez un son différent par un souffle absolument droit et sans vibrato et laissez-vous porter par cet autre style de jeu !

Con su brillo apacible y suave, evocador de la gentil luz proyectada por la Luna, la **piedra de Luna** dícese ser la piedra de los nuevos comienzos. En la India, la piedra de Luna ha sido siempre tenida en alta estima por las mujeres porque se piensa que acentúa las virtudes femeninas. Esta piedra reflexiva representa el ciclo del cambio y también tiene un efecto poderoso al calmar las emociones.

Busque un sonido diferente usando una corriente de aire absolutamente recta sin vibrato, ¡y disfrute al tocarla en un estilo distintivo!

20

Cool Blues

Sapphire – September

One of the most precious of gemstones, the **sapphire** is second only to the diamond! It has been mined in both India and Sri Lanka for many thousands of years and was worn by royalty as a protection from harm. Its rich hue was thought to suggest a pure blue sky, which encouraged divine favour and spiritual peace. The sapphire is known as the wisdom stone as it focuses and calms the mind – just what you need for your practice!

In the opening bars listen to the swing style in the piano, and work carefully with the rhythmical aspect of this cool piece. At bar 31 make your slur as smooth as possible.

*Als einer der wertvollsten Edelsteine steht der **Saphir** hinter dem Diamant an zweiter Stelle! Seit vielen tausenden von Jahren wurde er sowohl in Indien als auch in Sri Lanka abgebaut und von den königlichen Familien als Schutz gegen Schaden getragen. Von seiner prächtigen Farbe sagte man, dass er den reinen blauen Himmel andeutet, welcher göttliche Gunst und geistigen Frieden fördere. Der Saphir ist auch als der Weisheitsstein bekannt, da er den Geist konzentriert und beruhigt – also genau das, was du für dein Training brauchst!*

Höre in den ersten Takten auf den swingenden Stil des Klaviers. Arbeite in rhythmischer Hinsicht vorsichtig bei diesem coolen Musikstück. Spiele die Bindung in Takt 31 so weich wie möglich.

*Dans l'ordre des pierres les plus précieuses, le **saphir** suit immédiatement le diamant ! On l'extrait depuis des milliers d'années en Inde et au Sri Lanka où il était porté par les membres des familles royales comme protection contre tous les maux. On a rapproché sa teinte riche du bleu d'un ciel pur favorisant les exaucements divins et la sérénité spirituelle. Le saphir est connu comme la pierre de la sagesse qui concentre et apaise l'esprit. Exactement ce dont vous avez besoin dans votre travail !*

Ecoutez le style swing des premières mesures du piano. Soignez particulièrement l'aspect rythmique de cette pièce divertissante. A la mesure 31, liez le plus possible le phrasé.

Una de las más preciosas gemas, el **zafiro** viene solamente detrás del diamante! Se ha extraído en la India y Sri Lanka por muchos miles de años y fue usado por la realeza como protección contra los daños. Se piensa que su rica tonalidad sugiere el cielo azul puro, que anima el favor divino y la paz espiritual. El zafiro se conoce como la piedra de la sabiduría porque enfoca y calma la mente – ¡justo lo que usted necesita para su práctica!

En las barras del comienzo escuche el estilo swing del piano y trabaje cuidadosamente con el aspecto rítmico de esta fresca pieza. En la barra 31 haga muy bien su ligado.

22

Illusion

Opal – October

The ancient Romans used this iridescent stone as a symbol of power, and it was mined by the Aztecs more than 500 years ago. In seventeenth-century France the **opal** was thought to be unlucky: King Louis XIV named all his coaches after gemstones and the driver of 'Opal' was usually drunk and frequently crashed!

On a positive note, psychologically speaking, it is said that the opal amplifies traits and enhances self-worth, enabling the bearer to reach their full potential. It is associated with love and passion and, mentally, promotes lightness and spontaneity. Opal is also said to encourage an interest in the Arts!

Listen to the piano part of this piece. It is a little jazzy and will set the mood for the main melody.

*Les Romains de l'Antiquité ont élevé cette pierre iridescente en symbole de pouvoir et les Aztèques l'extrayaient il y a plus de cinq cents ans. En France, au XVIIe siècle, l'*opale *avait une image malchanceuse. En effet, le roi Louis XIV avait donné un nom de pierre précieuse à chacun de ses carrosses or le cocher de L'Opale était généralement ivre et faisait souvent verser sa voiture !*

D'un point de vue psychologique plus propice, l'opale est réputée souligner les qualités et grandir la valeur propre et, donc, aider celui qui la porte à réaliser toutes ses potentialités. Elle est également associée à l'amour et à la passion, à la légèreté et à la spontanéité mentales et favorise l'intérêt pour les arts !

La partie de piano en style de jazz installera l'ambiance appropriée.

Die alten Römer verwendeten diesen schimmernden Stein als Symbol der Macht, und von den Azteken wurde der **Opal** *vor mehr als 500 Jahren abgebaut. Im Frankreich des 17. Jahrhunderts hielt man den Opal für einen Unglücksstein. Der Grund war, dass König Ludwig XIV. alle seine Kutschen nach Edelsteinen benannte. Der Kutscher des „Opal" war normalerweise betrunken und hatte häufig Unfälle.*

Positiv ausgedrückt und aus psychologischer Sicht sagt man vom Opal, dass er Wesenszüge verstärkt und den Selbstwert anhebt, wodurch er den Träger des Steines zum Erreichen seines vollen Potentials befähigt. Er wird auch mit Liebe und Leidenschaft in Verbindung gebracht, und auf geistiger Ebene bringt der Opal Leichtigkeit und Spontanität. Man sagt ihm auch eine Anregung des Kunstinteresses nach!

Der Klavierpart ist ein bisschen jazzig und gibt daher die Stimmung vor.

Los antiguos romanos usaron esta iridiscente piedra como símbolo del poder y los Aztecas abrieron minas de **ópalo** hace más de 500 años. En el siglo diecisiete en Francia el ópalo se tenía por desafortunado porque rey Louis XIV nombró a todos sus carruajes después de piedras preciosas ¡y el conductor de "Ópalo" generalmente estaba borracho y su carruaje sufria frecuentes choques!

En una nota positiva, hablando psicologicamente, se dice que el ópalo amplifica rasgos y realza la autoestima, permitiendo al portador alcanzar su máxima capacidad. También se asocia con el amor y la pasión y, mentalmente, el Ópalo otorga ligereza y espontaneidad. ¡Se dice que anima el interés por las artes!

La parte del piano es un poco "jazzy" y reflejerá el humor de la música.

Golden Rays

Topaz – November

There are a number of myths associated with **topaz**. Some say that the word developed from the ancient name of an island in the Red Sea, Topazos (now known as Zebirgit); others believe that topaz derives from the Sanskrit word *tapas*, meaning 'fire' or 'heat'. It is said that topaz brings generosity, joy, abundance and good health. It aids problem solving and is especially useful for those active in the Arts. Another good flute stone!

Be very careful with the first accented notes and practice these alone first. Play with a big, full sound, paying particular attention to bars 6 to 9. The bars where you need more finger control should be repeated in your practice. Never be afraid to do repetitions and compare them – all the top flautists do!

*De nombreux mythes sont attachés à la **topaze**. D'après certains, son nom viendrait de Topazos, ancien nom de l'île de Zebirgit dans la Mer Rouge, tandis que d'autres le croient dérivé du sanscrit tapas désignant le feu ou la chaleur. La topaze est réputée apporter la générosité, la joie, l'abondance et la santé. La topaze aide à résoudre les problèmes et se révèle particulièrement bénéfique à ceux dont l'activité est tournée vers l'art. Encore une pierre favorable aux flûtistes !*

Portez toute votre attention aux premières notes accentuées et travaillez-les d'abord isolément. Jouez avec une sonorité large et pleine en soignant particulièrement les mesures 6 à 9. Répétez plusieurs fois les mesures exigeant la plus grande maîtrise des doigts. N'hésitez jamais à répéter certains passages et à mesurer vos progrès. Tous les grands flûtistes le font !

*Es gibt eine ganze Anzahl von Mythen, die sich um den **Topas** ranken. Einige sagen, dass sich das Wort aus dem alten Namen einer Insel im Roten Meer entwickelte (heute als Zebirgit bekannt). Andere glauben, dass er von dem Wort tapas aus dem Sanskrit abstammt, das Feuer oder Hitze bedeutet. Man sagt, dass der Topas Großzügigkeit, Freude, Überfluss und gute Gesundheit bringt. Er hilft bei Problemlösungen und ist besonders für jene nützlich, die in den Künsten aktiv sind. Noch ein guter Flötenstein!*

Sei sehr vorsichtig mit den ersten betonten Noten und übe sie erst einmal alleine. Spiele mit einem großen, vollen Klang und achte besonders auf die Takte 6 bis 9. Die Takte, in denen du eine bessere Fingerkontrolle brauchst, solltest du beim Üben wiederholen. Scheue dich nie, Wiederholungen zu spielen und sie miteinander zu vergleichen – alle Top-Flötisten tun das!

Hay un número de mitos asociados al **topacio**. Algunos dicen que el nombre viene del nombre antiguo de una isla en el Mar Rojo, Topazos (ahora conocido como Zebirgit), otros creen que topacio se deriva de la palabra *tapas* en Sánscrito que significa fuego o calor. Se dice que el topacio trae generosidad, alegría, abundancia y buena salud. Ayuda a solucionar los problemas y es especialmente útil para aquellos activos en las artes. ¡Otra buena piedra para la flauta!

Tenga mucho cuidado con las primeras notas acentuadas y practique estas solo primero. Toque con un sonido grande y completo mientras que presta atención particular a las barras 6 a 9. Las barras donde usted necesite más control de los dedos se deben repetir en su práctica. Nunca tenga miedo de hacer repeticiones y compararlas – ¡todos los flautistas lo hacen!

Sacred Song

Turquoise – December

The name 'turquoise' comes from *pierre turquoise*, meaning 'stone of Turkey'. This ancient gem has been mined in Nishapir, Iran, for about 3,000 years! Another well-known mining community was the Aztecs, an ancient civilisation of Central America, who used the stone as an offering to the gods. Nowadays, the south-western part of the United States supplies most of the world's turquoise. A thirteenth-century book on the virtues of the stone says: 'whoever owns the true turquoise set in gold will not injure any of his limbs when he falls, whether he is riding or walking, so long as he has the stone with him.'

Concentrate on a full sound, taking care with the rhythmical pattern and articulation.

Le nom de la **turquoise** *provient de la* pierre turquoise *de Turquie. Cette pierre ancienne est extraite en Iran, à Nishapir, depuis environ trois mille ans ! On l'extrayait aussi en Amérique centrale, dans l'ancienne civilisation des Aztèques qui l'utilisaient comme offrande aux dieux. Actuellement, la plupart des turquoises proviennent de la région nord-ouest des Etats-Unis. Un ouvrage du XIIIe siècle traitant des vertus des pierres stipule que: « quiconque possède une véritable turquoise sertie d'or ne se blessera aucun membre en cas de chute de cheval ou à pied tant qu'il portera la pierre sur lui. »*

Concentrez-vous sur une sonorité pleine en soignant les motifs rythmiques et le phrasé.

Der Name **Türkis** *stammt von dem französischen* pierre turquoise *ab und bedeutet Stein aus der Türkei. Dieser uralte Stein wurde in Nishapir, Iran, bereits vor ungefähr 3000 Jahren abgebaut! Eine weitere wohlbekannte Kultur, die Türkis abbaute, waren die Azteken, ein altes Kulturvolk aus Zentralamerika, die den Stein als Opfergabe für ihre Götter benutzten. Heutzutage liefert der südwestliche Teil der Vereinigten Staaten die größte Menge an Türkis in der Welt. Ein Buch aus dem 13. Jahrhundert sagt über die Vorzüge dieser Steine: „Wer auch immer einen echten in Gold gefassten Türkis besitzt, wird seine Knochen beim Fallen nicht verletzen, egal ob er reitet oder wandert, solange er den Stein bei sich trägt."*

Konzentriere dich auf einen vollen Ton und beachte die Rhythmusmuster sowie die Artikulation.

El nombre **turquesa** proviene de *pierre turquoise*, que significa la piedra de Turquía. ¡Esta piedra antigua se ha extraido en Nishapir, Irán, por cerca de 3.000 años! Otras fuentes bien conocidas fueron los Aztecas, una civilización antigua de América Central, que la utilizó como ofrenda a los dioses. Hoy en día, la parte sudoeste de Estados Unidos es la que provee la mayor parte de turquesa del mundo. Un libro del siglo trece en las virtudes de piedras dice: "quienquiera que posee la verdadera turquesa engarzada en oro no dañará ninguno de sus miembros cuando caiga, si él monta a caballo o camina, siempre y cuando tenga la piedra con él."

Concéntrese en un sonido completo, teniendo cuidado con el ritmo y la articulación.

S&Co.8106 Printed in Germany

Afterword...

I hope that you have enjoyed our journey through the cycle of gemstones as much as John Lenehan and I have enjoyed putting this special collection together. With all of the pieces, one a month, I hope that you have found exciting new ways to play your flute with your best sound and an added variety of colour.

Remember always to make a plan: plan your work and work your plan! It is a good idea to be able to play to someone just for fun – maybe family, flute friends or your class at school – so you have a chance to demonstrate what a 'little gem' of a flute player you are!

I would especially like to thank my assistant Catherine Ramsden for her invaluable contribution.

Elena

Postface...

Je souhaite que vous ayez pris le même plaisir à parcourir ce cycle de pierres précieuses que John Lenehan et moi-même à rassembler ce recueil très particulier. Au rythme d'une pièce par mois, sans doute avez-vous découvert de nouvelles façons de jouer de votre flûte, de produire votre meilleure sonorité et une plus grande variété de coloration du son.

N'oubliez jamais ce principe : planifier son travail et respecter son plan ! Il est toujours bon de jouer pour le plaisir devant quelqu'un, votre famille, des amis flûtistes ou votre classe et d'avoir ainsi l'occasion de montrer quelle « joyau » de flûtiste vous êtes !

Je remercie tout particulièrement mon assistante Catherine Ramsden de son aide inestimable.

Elena

Nachtrag. . .

Ich hoffe, du hast unsere Reise durch den Edelsteinzyklus genauso sehr genossen wie John Lenehan und ich das Zusammenstellen dieser besonderen Sammlung. Bei all diesen Stücken, eines pro Monat, hast du, wie ich hoffe, neue aufregende Möglichkeiten entdeckt, die Flöte mit deinem besten Ton zu spielen und dabei viele Farbnuancen hinzugefügt.

Denke immer daran, einen Plan zu machen: plane deine Arbeit und sorge dafür, dass dein Plan funktioniert! Es ist eine gute Idee, irgendjemandem einfach aus Spaß vorspielen zu können – vielleicht der Familie, Flötenfreunden oder deiner Klasse in der Schule. Auf diese Weise hast du die Möglichkeit, zu zeigen, was für ein ‚little gem'- Flötist du bist!

Ich möchte mich besonders bei meiner Assistentin Catherine Ramsden für ihren unschätzbaren Beitrag bedanken.

Elena

Epílogo. . .

Espero que haya disfrutado de nuestro viaje durante el ciclo de piedras preciosas tanto como John Lenehan y yo lo hemos hecho al juntar esta colección especial. Con todas estas piezas, una cada mes, espero que haya encontrado nuevas maneras de tocar su flauta con su mejor sonido y una variedad agregada de color.

Recuerde siempre hacer un plan: ¡planee su trabajo y trabaje su plan! ¡Es una buena idea poder tocar para alguien solamente por diversión – quizá la familia, los amigos flautistas o sus compañeros de clase en la escuela para así tener ocasión de demostrar que clase de "pequeña gema" es usted.!

Quisiera especialmente agradecer a mi asistente Catherine Ramsden por su invaluable ayuda.